CW01033184

Sweetdark

Sweetdark

poems

SAVANNAH BROWN

First published 2020
1st edition / *01*

ISBN: 978-1-5272-6892-0

Printed and bound in the United Kingdom
by CPI Group

Cover art by Agnes Cecile
Force of Gravitational Attraction, 2019

www.savbrown.com

to the sweetdarks i have known / will know / know

CONTENTS

III.

I remembered what had been circling in me: I am beautiful. I am
   full of love. I am dying.

Ada Limón

I.

VOID/YOU

here's what acquaints you with nature's dark apathy.
only a child, but one look at the atlantic in flux

is enough to know that's where you're meant to pitch your body,
primally, the truth of it written on some hidden artifact, ancient

and yours. do you know the weight of infinite stinging atoms,
the ones you want to love, bent on your destruction? you'll learn,

ribbony girl limbs pinned for a little lifetime to the sandbar,
your fresh reality that angry lunar rush, crushed chest, your spasming

lungs, tongue brine-sour, young panic. there it is: now you know love
doesn't cut it. followed by: now you know you can die. and what

are you gonna do about it, huh? first, surface, back into the bleached
midday. hack. the sun snaps above you, like fingers. stagger

out, pursued, little freckle-dusted seraph. mom brings the reckoning,
but it could've been anyone, a stranger, or what some people call

god. do you cry? which is you, which is sea? mom says *i won't
have you afraid of the ocean.* then she says *get back in.*

and you do.

it doesn't matter how, whether or not you shudder at the web-
toed chill or what it promises. if you don't remember,

you tread until sunset and the world doesn't end. years
pass, in their quick and unnoticed way. on your left hip,

a scar, tawny and grained, like martian soil, and what's left
to forgive? not the moon, the earthblood, the only blue being

into which you can slip unknown and unknowable—maybe
just as wronged. but the fear needs somewhere to go, intersecting

obliterations now round every corner, the silver magnetic mass,
formless, not creatable or destroyable, always churning—and where

is judgment day? i won't have you afraid of clock hands.
not of your own unfamiliar reflection. not the hapless lonely wander,

of your skull not as home but ivory cage, of your own pain, given pain,
needless pain—fine, then. again. go again, horizon-eyed. step into

the tide of a trillion tomorrows, crush below the wet and pulverized
mess spat by each frothing horror, and wade into the dark, like water.

WE ARE THE FLEDGLINGS

when even this lurid hour drops the leash—
that's how i know the night is going well.
there's no more left to lose. what sharps?
what aloof, protective mystery? what home?

the caper's third haunt, in one of those old
man pubs, our heads thrown back in the mahogany-
choke and mold colony, darts thumping,
tables sticky and seeping ale and fine, i'll play
sweetie, i'll play pet, i'll play love. if i blush,
and peach hasn't shouldered itself through the heavy
dim, have i blushed?

before i stand to reach you all, my thighs cling
to the booth leather and pop free.

the unvisitable place, which is not a place, which
is a feeling, which is an inimitable feeling—
hollering, self-wooing succubi—

a bottle shatters at the bar and i'm scared
to link our fingers in case it was really the collapse
of our own breakable thing, our tenderglass

worth naming but too weak to survive ultraviolet
gaze, obliterated by the rattle of one line
spoken too gently.

tell you what: i'd traverse the shards
barefoot to keep this going, then jar
the consequence as a souvenir.

after the yellow hours offer their timid
ought-to's we invent a new twisted
collection of sounds that fold themselves
into the wooden nooks, different words
for the same shriek:
we were here, so far from death.

THE UNIVERSE MAY STOP EXPANDING IN FIVE BILLION YEARS

at which point time will cease
to exist and i can finally stop
complaining. there's a fragile
world reflected in the glassy
pearl of your spit left
on my belly and i'm telling
you, i've never been so
old. the day sucks with leech-
teeth. even given the shreds
of your dead rind caked under
my fingernails there's the black
chasm of want expanding
in my chest the way a bead
of ink breaks, making me difficult
to touch without an exit plan.
imagine, please, a better
continuum. you say *earlier*
doesn't feel real and you're right,
not because there was anything
exceptional about the heath
in early afternoon, not because
our chins sticky with cider
was a notable pip in this

quivering glitch of a life,
but because it was too ordinary
to even dare remember,
because we'll someday ache
for any regular sunday in june
where the sun was a sure
thing and breath tasted like warm
grass and there was not a single
indication the cosmos would one
day shut like your eyes, tight
with pleasure.

TOO HOSTILE TOO TICKING

summer's corpse breath
has me whirring mad across the inanimate

bridge from canning town to the docks.
i'm less than nuisance. less than dust. there's passing

regard of the gut-knuckled wind, ricocheted
from half-scrapers and cranes and fellow

faceless travelers, which, yeah, if you need
to know, makes me think of the pavement

doused in the copper blaze of fantasy blood
spatter, like, i wanna snuff out some of that magic

god-given stuff with my hands, that's how bad
this is. the gossamer blot which begins in my gums

which is me but not me says everything is ruined
and it is. mouth rinsed in hot dread. i need to never

be touched again. i need every human body stacked
on top of mine, crushing. still, there's always light:

the tessellated dark matter, rootless stars and me,
on fire. quick, a riddle: which phenomenon

is capable of producing the fiercest rage, yet cares
the least about it? the walk home from the night

bus takes ten minutes and somehow
i don't appreciate a damned second.

THE DIFFERENCE

today the sun drenched
    a shadowless soul
spilt over with calm
    and beginning;

still it drifts in the non-place
    between the two:
feeling alive, and feeling
    like living

AN IMPECCABLE FUNCTIONAL DESIGN

you, doomless and new, shake out the sock
full of the once-forms of gastropods

and mollusks, soft animals, now softer,
left behind their permablacks, saw-toothed

manors of magnolia, sage, heather, pleated
peach and tangerine. i think of my own

biological paint: table cream, gunmetal,
the spent smear of oxidized copper scrubbed

from the sheets, the color of dirt—yes, fine,
i'm jealous of the dead things. i imagine the honor

of creating a keepsake with only with my body,
to leave behind, to be loved, long after,

and oh, we're back! here it rages, the rotten
horse which breaknecks towards my frontal lobe,

come to seek the sole rider. smack my lips
while i still can to rile the bitter tang.

adages of the voidal trance: oil your face
(flesh-death) and peel the orange (flesh-death)

and fuck (flesh-death-flesh, by the way,
did you know, inside you, you can grow

a whole story of pain?) look around,
there's never not a wrong organ, or something

sheathed in skin, something else to flay—
and that's how this goes, careening in the curl

of an infinity i've been told can't be hostile,
which doesn't explain the scars, or the purple fat

which drips onto my cheeks. gentleness is often
enough—a long, blue breath. you hold the shells

as if they don't belong to ghosts, so tame with what
you love. there's one shaped like a corkscrew,

arched brushstrokes tightened into a dense
central point, straining like a shut eye, coiled

into itself, no—itself a coil, and so i decide this
is merely the way of things, spiraling. *did you mean*

to say infinity, or just a very large number? before this,
we walked to the far green. you smelled like orange

peels on the way, and there were lilies with three
petals and buttercups five and cosmos eight

and perhaps always in tandem there's the certain
whirlpool, swirling on towards little oblivion.

IF I'VE EVER MADE SOMETHING BEAUTIFUL

i.

it wasn't on purpose. when the boy swears god
loves me i think *i have not even met the guy*
but sure, i'd like to, so this is how i'll spend
the impossible day, captive in a beater driving
down west market as he says *look at all of this*
gestures to a strip mall *and tell me you don't*
believe in a creator

ii.

consider superglue. unintended headway   penicillin
dynamite coca-cola champagne! wilhelm channels
a mystery ray and calls it x, not divine. a sparkling
current propels atom through atom, green disaster
blaze which deems the flesh extraneous, and the light
understands now. the broken particles, imagined,
dominated, even the intimacy too close as ghosts
of orderly black appear revealing what before
we'd had to bleed to know. sorry, sorry, what
had he been trying to do, again

iii.

i shouldn't have been so hard on the strip mall. what
am i asking of it? it's the point, anyway, that there's sin
and miracle nothing else, and hey, i clock a robin folding
branches into the *o*'s of the sign on goodwill, where inside
someone buys a stranger's blood-red confession
dress. i want the boy to define *accident.* then *mistake.*
for fun he'd rally *creation* and *discovery*, but look, i'd say,
don't you feel it, when the sun casts shadows across
the ugliest parts of you, the senselessness, the stumbling,
our tipsy sleepwalk into ourselves, in the same instant
formed and found, and i blink the wet eyes that happen
to bore down to the marrow, looking for god, and discover
two-hundred off-white flecks of rubble, of what the earth
built with what was left of heaven.

ENOUGH

no maybe the ugliest hours shouldn't host
miracles but still they go on hosting for example
this all happened while i was fumbling around

in the unnatural morning like a nocturnal
animal and you don't have to believe me
i wouldn't believe me but on the way home

the seagulls were laughing like kids

and i tipped my head to the day-moon which hung
translucent with a projection's non-reality against
a sky so blue my teeth chattered and when i lay

face down beside the brook i swore
the earth flexed against my belly a degree
of a degree of a degree of a degree of a

     crucial degree

act as though you've just been granted immortality
and i'll mirror the buzz. admit it, that's what it's like,
on golden-fluke mornings, or two glasses in, or dodging
the fidgety mayflies on erie, the day boiling fierce
in every direction. to be happy, sometimes, feels like
quitting. other times, only chemical, like when you brush
my chest so gently i assume you're looking for a hair-thin
seam, or which rough spine to tug and send the whole wall
spinning in the direction of the hidden things—suddenly
there's my heart, as bloody and heady as yours.
right now, we're still. chins tilted towards the trace
of distant pinpricks sewn in orange, gulls as antishadows;
concurrent focus, as if into the eyes of something bigger.
as if we are the eyes. i decide joy to be the natural state
of the cosmos, the return to it some kind of entropic
fate. my skin practically puckers. each taste bud, a name.
this is so beautiful and there's nothing i can do about it.
you are so beautiful and—understand, every night
the collective us sees seven billion sunsets. have you
even checked? really, really looked? say *earth*. know
the experience of saying it, how the letters together
behave like a cricket's purr, *earth,* that honeyed thrum,
earth, so easy to breathe, *earth, earth, earth.* i don't need
you to meet the rapt stagger. i don't even need you

to remember. just know, now—seven billion sunsets
and here's me, convinced we're seeing the same one.

AUTOPSY, PERFORMED GASPING

i would have never forgiven
myself had i stepped on that stag
beetle. stark maroonish bullet
hole, pincers scratching against
the pavement gentle as a whisper,
in the city!—

i tell you about him and vow
to start watching my feet.

there's no time to gasp before
before you save me from the drop
and haul me the rest of the way
over the fence. today i'm convinced
by my own humanity, so much
a person. maybe i've fallen for a trick,
my mind's protective char doing its job,
but hey, am i evolved or what!
meanwhile, the oaks ahead of us
unfurl like surgery curtains.

i'm thinking of a boy i remember
nothing about except his crime
when he, despite the girls'

pleading, slammed his awful
foot down onto the head
of what was once the praying
mantis, who popped like a berry,
all of this for no apparent reason
besides his having a foot
and her being there and our delicious
horror, and i never recovered
from the quiet racket her body
made, how substantial she appeared
at odds with how simply she died.

the daisies make space for us like a womb
and i keep telling you i could fall asleep.
what that means is i feel safe enough to lie
belly-up. what that means is this is unusual.

so it's known, that first night
i slept beside you, i didn't stir
a lick, not at all—

you untangle a branch from my hair,
clumsy and fond, and i know you weren't

supposed to see me like this. the breathing,
i mean. bacteria making a real show of being
bacteria, of the pins stuck in all my one
hundred thready legs, understand,
it's alleged that every eight
years my cells are made new
and so how will you know
that this me is the one you love?

(alternate ideas: me greater,
draped fleshless round forever
or just the ripples born by the skipped
rock and not the rock herself—
instead, in the underfoot brambles
unskipped and pathetic / everything
soft and chewy-pink / like this syrupy
grapefruit we tease apart when we
speak / like i want to rough anything
with you until it spits acid / your lips
curl around my shoulder and it snaps
like a cicada / how mechanical
the processes to accomplish tender
things / you scribble at the silky
spider bite i can't reach / i want you

to know that my hands tremble
like moth wings in a killing wind and)

there are still so many good
and steady ways to touch your face.

TELL ME LIKE YOU MEAN IT

before the worst of the red synapses cracks,
you remember the walls, and that no one knows
what it's like in there. you're trying to write

everything down. lay it out. endless three-card
solitaire, the canyon-gorged vinyls, every cursed
word you've let inside you which began safe

then grew, you've written them all, stony in the face
of obsession and rage, cuffed to the pursuit, lately,
of hobbies which promise to break skin, or slice

the pockmarks from the solitude. you love your nerves
twinged and the crimson drip beneath your tongue
that you can't drain alone. hey, tell 'em, suck

and it's like licking the bed of a lucky fountain, wish
and wish and gravestone, but taste isn't enough.
has never been. there's no story without your fingers

in their throat, so you're staring down the wellspring
and thinking of the telling, but even when you reemerge,
glowing and pruned, even after they've chewed

the miserable silt, you're still the only one
who's ever bruised their knees black, drunk as sin,
and you're still the only one who's prayed.

TRICK OF THE BLACK LIGHT

cackling   i'm thrust through the labyrinth
        of mirages   and powder,
headaches and   shadow-split hoopla, all
    by legs i've supposed to be mine.

                    artificial fog clings
to the echoing cavern of my throat and my jawbone
        stitches in line
tongue tied with lime and almond
                    salt   and

where the mist dissipates
            so many pale necks stuck out for the picking.

misfits sing in my blind spot   intonation pain-
        passion   girl-eyes odd with neon green
                and ultratime

fingers are all that's needed to usher further through the mine-
            field   pressed in the soft
                            pink above my elbows.

    in unexpected places
i like to think   *how did i get here*   followed by

this body   *i mean*   *how is it here*   and tonight
i've decided i'm doing a fine job at being
             a body   all full of drink and chip
      grease and its desire to please—

isn't she living! isn't she just! that manic
             aphrodite   *spreading all her good*
     living
          all over the walls

fooled!   this better face contorted
with pleasure   clever smoke and mirrors
    look closer
    and see the pitiless filth sessions   mulling
from place to pointless place in the house   ego
            death haze—

doesn't matter.
here   i   race the skittish avon   holy in the streetlamp
    halos   on the dirty ground
         climb these technicolor foothills   held held
   holding
    press glossy metal to my lips like a right lover
under night's nipping cover   alive and aliver   love red-

wrung muscles doing their welcome throb   and no one needs
          to tell me i'm doing it right,

                                        i know.   later i'll peel
myself
     from the earth   baptized in dew
               subdued by daylight   made different
different   if not new
          but that was me too   who howled
out dog days and dripped from the rafters

                                        who will someday turn
     her finest self into more   than a half-lie

II.

THE PARAKEETS WHICH FLY IN GREENWICH PARK

are ring-necked parakeets and are not supposed to be
here. they're all over london and no one's sure where
they came from but there's a rumor that in the sixties
jimi hendrix released a breeding pair like some deity,
avian adam and eve sent unchecked onto the metropolis
and now the descendants cry wild, hysterical vapors
of lime, all the tumbling earth green but them a different
sort—and they're perched above canary wharf as if
it's what they're owed. at the observatory i tease the descent
with my feet, forty-five degrees against the grain down
from the precipice, and the dirt is dry and sharp against
the heels of my hands, which hurts but i want it to. lately i
think mainly of my own hollow bones. maybe i'm more feral
than i figured, cherry flesh ripe, my instinct the pit. i'll let this
life spread me out like a sky. remember, even the sun wants us
dead. so worried about belonging when we're all tangled
in the celestial root: chaos wants for no one but i was
released, and for a time, survived.

VIEW INCLUDING CABLE CARS

glowing cherry strip-eyes
highlight the neatly spaced
robotic fist-bundles slinking
across spider wire; call them
omen-paths, a syncopated
ceasefire, stream of kinetics
spindling certain towards
conclusion like a mind,
then halt in unsustainable
conditions, unlike a mind.
i keep getting the sense
something big is going to happen
but it never does. the mechanical
worm of the dlr charges past
below, singular and disjointed
car-stars, parallel, mid-flight.
i swear i'm always waiting ages
for the train. from up here
there's always one passing.
these eyes swell with mild
and weary epiphanies. i'm
watching because who else
is at this hour and there is no

view unworthy of attendance.
apparently i'm the universe
observing itself but lately
i feel like a grub predating
other grubs, like, i can't look
in the mirror but i can stare
at the sun. no feeling goes unfelt!
including the one which suggests
if every one of these cars
tumbled into the black dock-
water i wouldn't even flinch.
every feeling. coffee's done
and i turn away and that's
when i hear the splash.

A GROWING THING

surrounded by the sloughed ribbons of me
                    i take the long way home and find you there,
                                                    girl.

          banner in a rioting wind,
    capricious little grouch
                          starved for something unknown
                to everyone, especially you—
                                    of course you're angry.

watch as you eddy the tadpoles
                thinking yourself some omnipotent god;
          from the pond skaters, the foxgloves,
                you'll accept prayers until lunch,

scent awash in green,

                          raking at tree bark knees,

          a growing thing.
it's you, really, in the murky water
                          and the mason jar—

you're a relic of a soil-buried epoch,
                phosphene-drenched kaleidoscope of days
                                    which yawn so deeply

they wrap round the other side,

        too dizzying to hold from anywhere but a distance

when we meet i hold your face in my hands

      (my face   your hands)

   you smile like swelling yellow spring and plead

      take me with you, finished thing

and how, then, can i not piece

                  myself back together?

she's wrong.

      still flowering, same baby-wrists encircled

   by blades of grass,

      same metallic ring of bird bones:

so how can i not look at myself

   (in the reflective universe behind our house,

     off the silver-tinged powder of august haze)

               and love her, too?

SPRING OF THE BODY

on the darkened strand, i'm still thinking
of the changes. a six-feet stampede into
charing cross, trail of smoke behind, or maybe
just breath, mingling with the iron-chill
and almost-frost. the wind hasn't let up

for weeks. now a character
in the individual series of our lives;
the wind! we keep acknowledging amongst ourselves
for no apparent reason. maybe to prove we all
have something in common. this morning,

i had no plans, but i spent the night wrapped
in piano keys and cobbles with mainly strangers
and to my rigid home-body, this feels like progress.
i'm past the point of thinking growth an up and up
act, more forward and back, undulating along vinegar

waves—occasionally, sprawled open-mouthed along
the supple rubble of the tide, crunching on grit-
teeth—always, out to waves again. occasionally flung
by unseen current near atmosphere where below is only
a frothed suggestion of somewhere i once might have

been, folded slow in the distance, sluggish cream
and sapphire static. add any more dimensions
and can i still call it growth? do i just age?
can i cast thought outside myself for once?
towards what? for who? am i ever not nose to knee?

fine, i've left the body to check, and there i am, small
and punctuating, the dot of a question mark the bakerloo
line completes, hooking me round to some kind of home.
like: what's this called, when we're sleeping three
to a double and i'm in the middle, somehow not

claustrophobic, somehow full of motion and space,
the proximity finally meaning trust instead of threat?
i don't check the mirror before i leave. act of peace,
not disdain. the circle line is populated by time
travellers while i'm still deep in yesterday

but don't worry, i'll catch up, and near trellik
it's suddenly future, the annual throng
of buttery daffodils straight like stickbugs,
like us, clambering somewhere through central,
our lips curled like theirs, too, round vapor-

death. i swear, yesterday, this was all ice-charred.
now, vernal varieties of tree budding whorled
and adolescent leaves and i can't help but think
of all the stems that have broken bedrock
while i was focused on getting things right, waiting

to be found. i breathe in through my nose and out
through my mouth and it's an incredible thing.

nothing howls, and
the cherry blossoms fold
white and crisp, like bedsheets

bedsheets,

or wine

RARITIES

acorn caps   plastic dinosaurs
leaves as big as my head   identical
pebbles stolen from the neighbors' flower beds
then train tickets   maps   fool's
gold   and eventually a palmful of small
pills. i tell the ghost figurines i've been trying
to populate a sort of living museum, each
victim of my love granted a wing, filling it my
challenge of knowing. pinned here, find recurring
dreams, conspiracy theories, their answer
when i asked them to take me to the worst day
of their life and describe the color of the sky:
sapphire paint and human hair and the rosetta
stone. can i worship what's mine? this is the problem.
i move onto folding moments into catacombs,
as if there are any noble or artistic ways to display
the curse of yearning. from the other side of this bullet-
proof glass, pretty people strung up easy, press
for information, hear them say *i need you* and *won't
you stay* and *will there be anything left of us,*
what a display, contrasted by the evening's
oddity, behold the semiprecious midnight spall

as curated by the sole keeper of the twilight babble.
and what's the point? these days not even
my breath is my own. if the words are profound,
let me let them be and let me let them go.
but i can't forget that the acorn caps are buried
in the woods behind my house and anyway,
you did think there'd be something left of us,
and i stamped that onto the damn moon,
and oh, how many times i've tried to slip
her into my pocket like a lucky coin—

OBSERVATION

rot lies with me in bed   clumsy stinking beast

who threads forever through   my lips

     and pulls   puppeteers

there's no place for me here   *prove me wrong*

         i should fear my heart both

     beating and still   *prove me wrong*

(here   a gasp shocks me awake)

only pain

        prove me wrong—

the sky does when   through a yawning

   grey wound it delivers

        a baptism   then

flecks of sunlight   which glint off the canal

   like diamonds   for no

      reason

FOLIE À DEUX

she winces at the kitchen table
            nails in thigh to bury the sting   says *you know,*
                        i don't think i was scared of death until i met you.

            i'm telling you, her blood's not clean,
      and if you drink it   you'll catch the same sick
                  (her honeycomb's sweet but your judgement
is sweeter)

                              no need to panic, but in panic we trust
it always gets the job done!

if one of you plays tapeworm,

                        the other is the sheep
      and you can lead a sheep to answers

                              but you can't make them think

here's the hot-lipped truth of it: everyone's sad,
                  don't think you're special. everyone's sad and scared
                  and everyone carries it around with them   wallets
            spilling over with wilted daffodils and finger bones—
everyone's got their own sludge. mix and you get into
                        the dangerous stuff, and this is bona fide
alchemy.
      weave thread through fermented pulp, wait for one violent

night to set the corpse waltzing then here's your new monster,
        frankenstein—appears it won't let you leave the house.

she eats the unlucky flies because she just wants you safe,
says   *i don't mean to project, but i'm pretty sure we're the*
only two people on this wretched planet who aren't on fire
so

> *why catch? it's so dangerous out there—*
> *why go? we have everything you could ever need*
> *in here. pull the blinds, darling!*
>   *they don't need to see*

IN ANTICIPATION OF THE HYDROGEN BOMB

in the worst of the hack-nasty visions
the walls are a stiff electric blue

and there are speakers which crackle
but don't tell me how to leave

you. after i choose to go the only way out
is through crooked circles of sterile hell,

and even the daisies turn away, and i'm crying
nylon wires, and i try to speak to the survivors

who don't know they're survivors but when
they open their mouths it's the horrible tinny

speaker-crackle that sputters down their clothes
like sick. everywhere a rotten siren follows me,

forewarning an inevitable event with a wail
no one else hears. if you made me, i'm all of

you. how do i repurpose every memory into
a memorial? i'm bad with my hands. i fear

unanswerable questions of self; like, what if
i ever muster up the courage to ask why i love

like a tourniquet? make the way i am make
sense. and this may be the secret of loss,

that despite my own continued presence in
the world i suspect that the slash

of a tether, more often than it frees,

                                    banishes.

ME, COVERED IN ASH

i'm belting around our quiet house like lashings
of rain again and no one hawks up any apologies.

what's it like to have to be everything i want forever?
fine, i'll start: sorry for the mugs i leave on my desk

for so long they develop their own ecosystems,
and for the weeks i eat badly, and the nights

i drink too well, for all these small and lumbering
ways i suggest none of this is enough. only the calathea

sees me careful and doting and this is proof there are
just some living things i care to keep living.

a no-turn lighthouse defying purpose, one stubborn
beam of yellow on mutinied black sea, strong enough

to suck up every last drop, sooty remnants of desire
left smeared on your cheeks that i try to clear

with yet another beacon until the hardwood's cooked
with rage and pitchy delirium. orange oven flaps its maw

like an invitation. and you're there, saying *your obsessions*
will be the death of us, and the fear, and those awful

dreams that hang around for days, and i don't know why
i show only the people i love my ugliest self. even when

the bedroom is warm and the peace lily's
blooming and the cat, perched near the ceiling,

tuts at the magpies hopping along the canal you'd
think, at last, there's nothing left to lack, but that's

the kicker, there's always something left, and none
of it's real. i don't want to admit to the dare:

keep on loving this, do it, and see if i care.

FIFTY-TWO BLUE

for a second   imagine a different kind of wilderness.
cobalt mist   sizzling through the full bare
whooshing currents   light forever muddied
and everywhere refracted. another year   then another
returned as the ghostly lone rumble on the hydrophones
no mechanical whir   /   soviet submarine   just
                    you   you, flying solo
come down again from the kodiak like a prophecy singing
that solitary hymn. there is no language for one.   i'm
speaking directly to you now: we'll bond over your
aloneness   recognize our own bloodshot geyser-eyes
remembering   all the poems we didn't read to each other
and how many times we could have said love and blue whales
known for their strong and enormous hearts   commonly
live in the wild one hundred years and sometimes at home
i worry about being misunderstood   / my phone
is lighting up and i don't answer   / my ankles are soaked
and rusted anchors / i'm wondering if i'm better off dry
on the pavement muttering *anyone anyone anyone* waiting for
someone to coax the mutual song of being from my throat so
for a lifetime   imagine a different kind of wilderness.

III.

BLOODSUCKER

dad tells the story: ohio deepwood, him and his brother
little league helmet-clad, tossing stones into the inky sky
until a bat, gravity-lashed, swoops down in their wake,
thinking the ordinary shapes horseflies or sweat bees or hawk
moths, and yes, i can imagine the thrill when the whip
of wind cracked past their necks, when the promised pain
just missed, but i still have a gnawing sort of pity for any
other creature who darts towards the first shrouded wonder
moving in the dark, who throws its whole self at hunger without
fear of breaking teeth, who hopes the wonder might keep it
alive, who doesn't know, or hasn't considered, that every restless
shadow exists only to watch something want.

EARTHLY PLEASURES!

hysterical lightning thrashes across taut
nitrogen-skin, instantaneous yellow rivers
reflected in the wetness of your face.
i imagine the quick veins sticking in place,

the fractals seared into the atmosphere,
which, if we're lucky, might break apart
with a flash, tangy and deliciously irate—
fine, i understand every wretch who's fallen

in love after seeing me angry. we've been
watching for ages. another marvel ruined
with overindulgence, aggressively consumed,
like unearthing a plot of oxeyes and junebugs

with a toothy grab-crane—but i can't pull
myself from what makes me a clever animal,
addicted to the snappy brag of what's above us
and the next bite of fear that sends me giggling

like a stream. i recite reality in preparation:
if that's the last strike then that's the last strike.
later we spell need on the other with our hands,
me your external racing heartbeat,

and with my head thrown skyward
there's the biggest crash yet, a real glass-
smasher, skeleton-wringer, so near that
the room goes dark and the smoke

alarms cackle like courting blackbirds, so near
that i wonder if it had been birthed from me,
and i'm howling at the thought, and all the while
you're watching, parched and expectant and wanting

more, and i'll tell you until those white-hot stars
split that there's always something more.

IMPACT

i can see it already: us pressed between sheets
of paper towel to draw out any remaining moisture.

iron on low for fifteen seconds, careful not to burn then
slide us into a deathless album of your choosing. you

taught me that, how to crush pastlives into wrinkled
husks. this all started because your dad had a boat docked

in super-sargasso and i can't resist the sea, so i tag along
and spout my pretty gibberish. muffleheads multiplying,

behold me rolling in the dizzy loaming peaks, clothed
in only green foam, attention afforded from infinite tongues

icy-hot with cinnamon gum wound around your pinkie
until circulation cuts. let me show you my soft company.

i want to be your girl, in the same way you hold the glistening
body of mars in a telescope's lidless eye and say she belongs

to you; swivel the lens and she's gone in the dark, thirty
million miles away and blushing. my earthly familiar,

my medicinal dose of casual serotonin, you've answered
the big questions: can i be even more alive? can i love

even less? we leave once i've seen all of you, palms
upturned, your edges as blurred as our planet

from pre-space, then take the highway home where
the lamps loom as if they're the growths of enormous

anglerfish and i'm thinking, somehow, that this splinter
of time maims deeper than eternity, and i'm too scared

to tell you i don't know what to call this thing reproducing
between us, like the deer who doesn't know the name

of the roaring and luminous beast flying through the black,
only that it's getting closer and closer and closer.

LOW-LEVEL ANNIHILATION

does it matter, really, for what reason
the matches are struck?
sometimes i light them only to snort

the ceremonious sulfur as transport
back to one of the few-candled birthdays,
of anything being worth celebrating,

a nascent year, outrageously long, stacked
like a wreath instead of a breezeblock.
i mean, what's the most important

fate-pawn i could have burned,
or the most wonderful aftermath
as a result of its burning? or maybe

the meaning is the licking flame
itself, young and orange, a wriggling
newborn. or, no, not like a newborn,

sorry, i've just been thinking about—
or an empty prism, you say, from
the negative space. right. without

the activating glint it may as well
be any other glass. *or anything else
at all.* if purpose is a moment

and not a monument then all
there is to do is keep writing
things down. i want to make

something with only my mind
that glows well enough to warm
you. *fireflies, you'll find, are cold*

to touch. tell me this is what's intended:
this brief parade of stubborn
heat, this dream of sparkling light.

EGO

mom tells me if i keep up these stormy episodes,
my face will be stuck like that, an unending tempest.

i'm wrestling with myself in the fireplace when
i realize i don't know what i look like. not really,
    not under duvet or water or lousy
    with moonrays, and i don't know which is most me:
    to be daughter or lover or god to dependent plants.

at home, i'm weaving together my most vague
and delicate twine, whispering every word
that could set the buds burning red with need,
  try me   try me   try me.
lighting the candles with only my mouth.

i want to be the sum
  of only my most beautiful parts. this is wrong
of me but i can't decide why. i guess i've never writhed
  without awareness of the writhing—

    try anguish, then. try crumpled fly-girl throbbing in poison
    ivy. but even agony has dimples, and if the face is too honest,
    who would admit to love what's left, the bare and groping
    creature of legs or light or unspeakable mold?

if the wounds won't heal, become a wound.
i undress and expect to feel more naked,
or to reveal something before unnoticed:

    a harvestman's nest. a wormhole
        in the eye.

imagine becoming a girl ordained,
  some bilateral symmetry slicing
its way through the unbroken immorality.
i want any scrap of proof
  i'm supposed to be here,
        acting ridiculous.

there's a sensation i'm after: myself
    poured both into and all over myself.

if i still went to confession, i'd admit
  that sometimes when i flicker so full
of volatile want between your eyes
  in midmorning, sun at its most relentless,
i'm just looking for my face dunked
  in the oil of your pupils, the only place
i recognize her so well that my mouth
  parts slightly and stays there.

ME, BAREFACED, IN THE SYCAMORE

i'm smiling in the picture. that's the end of it.
but i'm picking the scab: swaddled in the knotted hammock
big enough for all three of us, my eyes are skewed and small,
jaw wobbly and missing, biggish shoulders hunched,
mostly unlit and sheened with sweat, like a grey sort of glass
smeared with the greasy bruises of our fingertips. i am my own
obscene cloud. i immediately hate myself for the thought.
after all, that was just one second, one imitation face.
and do you know what we did that day? we slunk through
blue wildflowers and tall grass, spoke of revolutions
and inconceivable faraway epochs and outer space.
it was summer again. daisy chains for everyone and i mean
everyone. peace and ball games. a sloppy bumblebee slept
in a pollen stupor. abundance in abundance. sweat means
the body is at work with the sun. when i look again i'm different—
unthinking of how or why the muscles move, just happy
that they do, able to climb. and if there was ever a place
i didn't need to be beautiful—

PROMISE

when the constellations separate / and instead spell out
future horrors / when the future is a sewn mouth / when
the earth is a flattened disc / when the stringy dark
screams back / when the crows break against the wind-
shield / when the past is sealed with the clean
fucking wax-teeth of all the starving eastern whip-poor-
wills / when the oceans ascend in a wall of jittering
droplets / when nothing has gone the blue and human
way we wanted / when another blameless robin goes
unborn / when the brain is a knot of barbed wire / we
pick / and pick / and pick / here's what i'll do / i'll say
goodnight / lover / see you in the morning / and it's
always true / believe me / believe me / forget everything
i've said / it's all wrong / don't trust a lick of it / except
this / goodnight / goodnight / the sweetness is coming

I WANT YOU TO LOOK AT THE MOON

(written only with words & phrases from quotes by the astronauts of the apollo missions)

realize, not even the garden
of eden is infinite. make
these impossible molecules
live for more than a moment.

    in the body, there emerges
    an intense dissatisfaction:
    is this it? are we so delicate?
    high up, freedom associated

with the absence of home,
the sparkling darkness
of space; in a different
world, the veiled crater

    of my neck, flushed with
    sunlight. we're too young
    to understand that we're
    too young to understand.

all of us, i mean. i touched
with one hand the ancient
mystery of the heavens,
sky-blue—and look at that!

i'm really here! i'm really
here, quite close to you.

ON THE LAST DAY, I CAN'T HELP

but be giddy. leave the bed unmade, the books scattered
spine-side up. chores are outdated. still, feed the cat.

how's the air? celestial orange. my cheeks round and red
and full of blood. the heat reminds me of how ends wear

the same clothes as beginnings, those shimmering midwest
days that stunk of chlorine, how the sun was two fists

clasped together. tune into stereo radio only: confessions of
love, accidental unsaids, prayers to the warm god. the frequency

whines like a skinny dog and we're quick to silence. no, no
one goes hungry. future stares into us as an accelerating wall

of eyes, a locust swarm. the past is a ball we toss between
hands. do you wield dual guns? not me; i won't spend my last

moment looking away. drink while there's time. has to be ziggy
on the speakers. i'm thinking of what's unresolved: aliens, peace,

those unidentified sounds bellowing from the bottom
of the ocean. a lack of conclusion is a conclusion. closure

is a manmade phenomenon. i imagine we go to a hill,
a cliff, altitude to give us the illusion of bigness. i'm vast,

i know it, and the cliff will be full of strangers with the same
delusions of grandeur, which means we'll get on like a cliff on fire,

and if you don't love them yet you will by the end of this. who'd
have thought, everyone both viewing and participating in the finale!

the real finale, one we can't review. for once i'm sure the best
has come, no second guessing, no mystique in the transference

of state, no hidden away soul or sound or synapse,
the simultaneous icy tinnitus, delighting in mutilated shapes,

those synchronized chants, all of us at once saying what a show,
truly, what a show this has been, and the applause is deafening,

and the lights are so bright, and the sky is a pit, and i am a pit,
and what's ahead is a pit, and we're all there, gnawing

at the air with our perfect teeth, and we all go
out and we all go down, and for once,

at last, we're all singing the most
common song

and

   later,

      a bulb

      yawns

         unobserved

MY OWN SMALL RUIN

i.

honestly, who knew that the rolling molten
pit of silvery nothing was something to fear?
fear of the insatiable curiosity, before that.

truth is god. the news lies but it is news. a trillion
more of these sinew-streaked liars
still to arrive, a billion years foreseen

but one hundred left if they're lucky
to clamber over one another like foam-blown
sand grains as the sea levels rise. i'm left choking

on the bled conjecture of how they might repent—
at the unfeeling knell of storm and eye and storm
and eye, what will the bottle-necked beasts

do when they find they've done the hurdling,
now nose-to-nose with grey-faced armageddon?
did they do it to themselves?

ii.

what, then, do i do with the even smaller

marvels? impossible. phenomena like eyelashes
and the fleshy fold of a throat from a word

swallowed, and quiet breaths taken alone.
mere and gentle curiosities. wanting, being
wanted, fabulous distractions. when you were gone

at the edge of the world and too green to ask,
i imagined the gradient of dawn as seen by you,
the white slates of spacelight on the contour

of your cheek, if the fire you roused had my eyes,
if when you laid to commune with the earth
the ground was too swollen to be anything

but bloodsoft flesh. i worry i've wasted finite
neurons on the puzzle but there's no minor
disquiet when there's the same attention

paid to all cosmic debris:
every light going out,
my lips pinched between teeth

given the fact of our feet, smoothed like pond
stones by the erosion of checking you're there, how
can i relax? so many conditions satisfied to catalyze
this action alone. two of us breathers who want
to know the other's opposite. you / i could be anywhere
but i am / you are here. *think bigger.* we could be anyone
but we're us. *bigger.* we could be anything besides
bipeds, feet for the checking. *bigger.* anywhen,
then! how easily the universe could've denied me
my kicks but here's this miraculous everyday,
truly large numbers crackling between the sheets
like eggshells—bring me back to now. i'm begging.
you'll notice everything's blooming, the short night,
the film of purple wine on yesterday's mugs
and even, i think, you. easy, easy: realism bites
destiny. no allowance for fate in these unspoiled
cuts of time. rip the halos from the stats, little-bliss,
it's just us down here. there is nothing romantic
about me reminding you of the big bang.
there is nothing romantic about me at all. you're
asleep and none of this occurs to you. pry open
your stung-red eyes and call me what i am,
which is nothing, and at this moment, the only eon

you've ever known, and i'll be brought back to now
no now   no *now*   where i'm humming
like a strum blade and soft as a petal and at least
until morning, the nearest miracle to your mouth.

A MEMORY

my picture of the apocalypse was perhaps unimaginative
and extraordinary. foreseen solar flare? sure. listen, worlds
end every day. uncountable amounts of destruction
since the first page. little deaths, too, too small to even tally.
loss webs between all moments, everywhere a space
where something once lived. here's my real worry:
i find myself at the brink of being's quiet crystalline
stream, the estuary emptying into the pool of all things
and non-things, and the synapses won't want to quit,
and my mouth will still be wet with bubbling atoms,
 and i won't be able to bring myself to kneel in the clay.
i've done so little living. how could there possibly be someday
more to lose? lie to me. tell me that in some faraway
future history of humanity, someone like me notices
this attempt at goodness, any of our exploits, any of those
golden hours where we had everything and nothing hurt—
is it too much to hope to be reanimated in the brain,
the tendril wrapped around a cortex? but there's a whole
rolling world for my myth to attend, and on one of those
indigo nights, there will bound an unusually playful
star, or a ripple of air otherwise headed home which jerks
like a peal of laughter to the sea, or a raindrop which takes
the shape of a hummingbird, or a second hand of a clock

which halts in place for an imperceptible instant
and bends a little at the elbow, suddenly remembering.

The epigraph by Ada Limón comes from the poem "After You Toss Around the Ashes" from her collection *Bright Dead Things*.

"i want you to look at the moon" was written only using words and phrases from quotes by Apollo astronauts Buzz Aldrin, Neil Armstrong, Alan Bean, Gene Cernan, James Irwin, Edgar Mitchell, and Alan Shepard.

"impact" references Charles Fort's Super-Sargasso Sea, the fictional dimension where lost things go.

The title of "this too shall devastate" comes from the adage "this too shall pass."

My endless thanks goes to my readers, whose unwavering support and patience is directly responsible for this book being able to exist at all. Thank you for being here, whether it's again or for the first time.

I'm so grateful for all of my teachers, but I need to especially thank Nathan Singleton and Kathy Zagar, who nurtured my love for words and demystified my goals at a time where a shred of discouragement might have sent me reeling. They will never not be present in what I write and I will owe them forever.

The biggest of kudos to editor Rhiannon McGavin for her invaluable insight and expertise. Thank you for making every poem better.

Thank you to my agents Richard Pike, Matthew Harvey, and Allison Howard for your support and for continuously making impossible things happen.

Thank you to Agnes Cecile, who very kindly allowed her art to be used on the cover—I couldn't have dreamt of something better suited.

I'm so appreciative to Connie, Patrick, Rosianna, Holly, and Melinda for their time, guidance, and notably, generosity. Familiar others know who they are.

Thank you to Bert for your dogged encouragement and for weathering my moods better than I do.

My dad instilled in me a fascination with stories. My mom did actually force me back into the ocean. These are maybe two ways to say the same thing, which is love. I'm so glad to have you both.

Savannah Brown is the author of the poetry collection *Graffiti (and other poems)* and novel *The Truth About Keeping Secrets*. Her second novel *How to Disappear* is forthcoming with Penguin Random House UK. She grew up in Ohio and currently lives in London.

You can find her at @savannahbrown on Twitter and @savbrown on Instagram.

ALSO BY SAVANNAH BROWN

Poetry
Graffiti (and other poems) (2016)

Novels
The Truth About Keeping Secrets (2019)
How to Disappear (2021)